ÍKAROS

By the same author:

Books

Gallery of Antique Art (2016)

Burnt Umber (2016)

Watching the World: Impressions of Canberra (2015) (with Jen Webb)

Six Different Windows (2013)

It Feels Like Disbelief (2007)

Blood and Old Belief: A Verse Novel (2003)

Stepping Away: Selected Poems (2001)

Canvas Light (1998)

Shadow Swimmer (1995)

The Dancing Scorpion (1993)

Acts Themselves Trivial (1991)

Chapbooks

Colours: Blue (2017)

The Taoist Elements: Earth (2016)

Jars (2015)

Viscera (2014)

Chicken and Other Poems (2012)

Mapping Wildwood Road (1990)

ÍKAROS

PAUL HETHERINGTON

Íkaros
Recent Work Press
Canberra, Australia

Copyright © Paul Hetherington 2017

All rights reserved. This book is copyright. Except for private study, research, criticism or reviews as permitted under the Copyright Act, no part of this book may be reproduced, stored in a retrieval system, or transmitted in any form by any means without prior written permission. Enquiries should be addressed to the publisher.

Cover illustration: Ornithopter and creator George R. White at
                        St. Augustine, 1927
Cover design: Recent Work Press
Set in Bembo

recentworkpress.com

ISBN: 9780648087861 (paperback)

A catalogue record for this book is available from the National Library of Australia

For Suzannah

Contents

Íkaros at the freeway's edge   9

Íkaros on land   7

Íkaros in flight   27

Íkaros and the mermaid   47

Íkaros on shore   59

Íkaros as refugee   79

Íkaros at the freeway's edge

1.

The crowded freeway runs like Lethe, night populated by plumed ghosts and singed, blear light. I press my hands together and my body is nameless flesh. Self is a crowd circling an empty arena. Thought is a thousand shouts and guesses. Cars turn toward the mountain.

2.

Like a stick in the throat I remember 'Íkaros'— my father's epithet. Arms that propelled, wings that ensconced. I've fathered myself for the thousand decades since pulled from the sea by an Italian witch. She hauled me like a casket, dragging me free of my wings. 'Are you really a bird?' she asked. 'Are you a boy dreaming of Leda? Will you become a downpour of gold?'

3.

The witch restored my body, that worms had digested; my stories sifted in their primitive guts. I'm not sutured well in this afterlife—made of songs that disperse on wind, the bloodied floor where the Minotaur danced.

4.

She parlayed me into granite, in a country she called the Antipodes—and, yes, I was there for interminable years, drinking oblivion from gasps of air. 'You'll wake', she said, 'in a few millennia. The world you know will be mere supposition and you'll feel your lack like evisceration.' And so I do, earning my keep, learning machinery's rhythms and noise. I have no provable self. The Minotaur's jabber returns to possess me.

5.

Memory ransacks me as my wrinkled story stands in that boy's future.

6.

Íkaros lolling like a painted figure in curling light
—can that be me? Íkaros watching a cat chase a
dog; burying feet into snarls of grass; peering into a
henhouse's clamour; crossing swampland; quizzing
words that name and possess him—'boy', 'son' and
'uncouth child'. Scrutinising a handsaw, imagining
a ladder inside the sun.

Íkaros on land

7.

Shadowed Ariadne dawdles with thread and won't catch my eye. What we discovered of one another hasn't adhered—and the Minotaur chases our wayward thought. Pasiphaë chastises and asks her to stand. My father, Daedalus leans into anger. Girls vault bulls. Meat tips from plates.

8.

My father dreams of a world of machines—horseless chariots, bird-winged men. He describes cities with insect eyes, continuous noise, pictures that walk. He foresees the end of Minos' kingdom in spilt earth and infantry-rushes of water. Minos scoffs. They face each other like penned bulls.

9.

Soldiers arrive, tapestries are taken: 'you'll have no luxury'. Empty mornings and derision's finger. My father instructs the evening: 'we'll find an exit.' He will not hold me but turns and turns through the room. A faceless moon climbs.

10.

We stand against our thoughts of a future and it blows like wind. The present is a wall pressing our backs. My father's vainglory is thin in his mouth; his brilliance now an ornate cage, as narrow as Danaë's. And no god appears to set us afloat on the bronze-like sea. We knock cups. His silence thickens. I say 'make peace'.

11.

We offer prayers and sacrifice. Yet something is damaged. The Minotaur knows it, refusing to eat. Ariadne leaps over a bull and is gored. Minos debauches himself. My father nods. Weeks stretch, as if the sun has slowed and the moon dawdles. My father refuses to burn our candles. Each night's a lather of stars.

12.

I think of Ariadne's wounded thigh. My father screeches like a gull.

13.

Dreaming with open eyes, I see the heavens roiling and churning. There are starbursts and collisions. A palette knife's smear reddens the sky. Dreaming with closed eyes I feel a rush of air like a coat pulled from my shoulders. A bird beaks companionship as if it's my brother. There's a rain of contradictory words. I shrink into a painted sea that feels like death, fixed with pigment and oil.

14.

Only in learning the Minotaur's babble did I come into speech. A word, and then three. A sentence or two. At four I spoke in paragraphs and my mother, Naucrate, cried. Now, no words will do. I push a few from my mouth and hold her shoulders. Her eyes burn fiercely against my misjudgments as she breathes like a cornered fox. I stammer and bark.

15.

Though the Minotaur resisted, we nestled into each other's light. My feeling pressed a narrow passage. Then Ariadne went to him at night as he jabbered through his dance routines. She seemed in thrall, promising favours. To watch him was to see beauty falling from his body in a lustre of movement. If he'd been able to speak clearly, what would he have said as we stood eye to eye?

16.

Ariadne walks with me by the river and points out stars, asking how we might escape. The Minotaur bellows in anger. Twelve guards chain him; my father shrugs; Ariadne unrolls her clew and consoles his anguish. In these last days he's a sun in that darkness, his lucent body inimitable.

17.

I dislike the name Íkaros, and its absence on my lips grows larger. To speak truly requires a new lexicon—knowledge won't speak with my tongue even as the Minotaur's prattle recognises me. My father dresses me in nouns that don't adhere. He insists on studiousness. 'Quell your restlessness,' he says. Within my mouth, latitudes of silence.

18.

Words are lead weights, an uncomfortable ballast (others I hold in my mouth like ruby sweets). Thoughts are ropes to pull me down. I tease them into gossamer threads to tie myself to the air. The sun's a hero I conjure to steal me from stacked, unwieldy days. This tower room surveys our anticipation.

19.

There's a ruminating doubt, like a slipstream—
that Íkaros might step free of clumsiness; that
the sun will free me of the need to hoist that
name; that feathers will make me a bird; that
flight will namelessly possess me.

20.

I see dissolving blue, try to imagine myself as a cloud. My father's gift of foresight reveals cities lit in neon, a thud of building, horns of wide river boats and a litter of affluence—where grass undulates next to clean water and a small flock skirts the mountain. A man like Minos struts in power and death's a black mushroom in his eye. Knowledge flexes in his hands.

21.

Time's a dropped bowl. As it splashes on the floor, I feel a twinge of the future. A vision of a sun ball; a gap I enter; sentences squeezing my speech.

22.

Holding Ariadne's waist, watching her let the bowl go. Seeing tracts of space in the blood clot of my eye, fatherless, my future tightly about me. The bowl sprays—a mermaid's image.

23.

My father gestures like a nocked arrow, as if no longer himself. He places his arms on my shoulders, quivers, murmurs something I miss, kisses my forehead. Yet his gaze isn't trained on me, travelling blind reaches. 'Here,' he says, 'unknowable boy', presenting a feather.

Íkaros in flight

24.

'It's time,' my father says. 'Hold yourself firm and remember your lessons.' He tightens straps. 'Stand upright, possess yourself.' My language is bound, the balcony's vista gapes.

25.

We look at each other, inspecting our surprise.

26.

Wings pull. Hand over hand we climb.
Feathers and wax crack the thick light. 'Lift,'
he says.

27.

A beaking seagull teaches me fall and swerve.
We're twins—flares of soft feather in a
thermal's upthrust. 'Like this,' the bird cries,
climbing until our prison is a pin in Crete's
brown cushion.

28.

I watch the skein of myself as if it's mist;
as if I'm a painting hung on air—a purple
abstraction. My heart a dangling basket.

29.

A camp for fugitives, guards, circling birds. Recollections haze me: my mother dips a cup, my father snatches it from me; we're on a long road walking in silence, where birds weave the sky with colours. A girl has her hand on my leg, a woman steals my purse in a market. Mountains and their pathways; a cave fronted by berries; a teetering hut. Running with the young Minotaur.

30.

I'm nearly stalled. Between wind-made walls the thrusts of breathing. Within wide sight lines, the idea of a tunnel. My father's distance startles. His contraptions clutter my arms; his language trickles.

31.

The sun's an orange on a blue plate, an eyeball quizzing me, an unreadable paean.

32.

The taciturn sky takes hold. My companionable bird drops. Daedalus is an irascible black fly. Sun speaks in hissing tones, on pulleys of light.

33.

I'm a lather of rays. The sky's wide room compresses. A hawk is the wind's spasm. Hand over hand, I swim towards a red buoy. Arm over arm I'm gifted the dawn's soft brilliance. Hour after hour I know myself as pained and panting flesh. Ariadne's black hair curls on my face as I play truant, visiting the Minotaur's hoofed chanting … thought turns me through a thousand hours. The wind asks, 'How has this happened?'

34.

I'm feather and waxed stitch. My words are a gull's interjection, my body a rocking counterbalance. Here, a metaphysics of the in-between; here, language as long elasticity; here, love as a cry draped on a mountain. I throw the trinket Ariadne gave; cast away my obedience. Touch leaves my fingers; injunctions are ballast I let fall.

35.

A high thermal twists me like something thrown and, like a boy trying to stone the sun, I concentrate on my dream's burning eye. Happiness overcomes. Then, like a pebble at the top of its arc, I have no grasp on air.

36.

I'm too many people. One climbs into the sun to dwell there. One drops to the ocean to gather pearls. Another lives in the tower. A fourth hears the rip of wings. A fifth is a Cretan farmer. One's a story told centuries hence. Another is a painterly splash in a sea.

37.

The letters of my name fall, and the detritus of thought. The scrabble of a thousand intentions fall, and imprecise locations of self: the alphabet and structure of every learnt taxonomy falls. I'm a particle cloud, momentarily becoming 'Íkaros'.

38.

My feathers are filaments, shape is stretched.
Eardrums fail. I'm rain, snowfall and gust.
I'm an anonymous song, a trailing ladder, a
comet with fading tail.

39.

In purple light like bending metal, flamed and distorted, there's no before or after. The Minotaur's kneading caresses redden my arms; Ariadne's mixed endearments curl. Bull-leaping games are a brutal pantomime. The ocean opens its mouth.

40.

Like hands cupped under a falling stone, so the sea crests. My wings are no better than a chicken's thin down. As once I felt a pebble slip between fingers, so I slide into the fingerless sea.

Íkaros and the mermaid

41.

The sun strips my feathers, singeing my cheeks. I tumble away from its whispers, hearing a thousand expletives.

42.

Water sucks me. There's a mermaid climbing shafts, dark rafters of shadow, fish plying coffin-cold blandishments.

43.

I see lobsters and gliding fish. Rocks approach, and strange glimmers, like the Minotaur's eyes. My name is a flat worm.

44.

Slow-crawling through ocean I see games in the gymnasium, my father bringing a castle of sticks, slaves lifting and holding, arms rising and shovelling, a girl with sharp nails, a jostling boy.

45.

The mermaid talks in oceanic currents. Hands take hold, as if death's a masseur. My mouth is sealed with undrowned air.

46.

As warm thought travels through a severe metaphysics, so we climb icy passages. Currents flare; fish with white lanterns taste me. The mermaid's fins open blips of seeing.

47.

Finding a scratch of sand and wheeze of air like saturated sky. Fronds that tear in a clouded wash.

48.

We lie in aftermath, my fingers shape her torso like an attic sculpture. Her heartbeat doubles my own. I cannot see her.

49.

She lounges in graceful gurgles that must be words.

50.

Slowly I clarify. Water soughs and wanders.

Íkaros on shore

51.

A witch meshes my broken parts. She laughs at a story that extrudes from my nose like Enkidu's worm. Her fingers open my gargling throat.

52.

Guessing myself to be dead, I look for a vista but see only darkness. I sense ocean and spume, a land with daubed huts, a herd and a shepherd, but cannot see them. Thinking myself dead, I ask what I know—whispers from school books, my father's arcane magic. Believing myself irredeemable, I quiz belief—there are bull motifs, my resistance. Wind feels like water. Tears are last squeezings of self. In my mouth a shout might be exultation. I recollect the Minotaur's stamping. I hear my mother's name as if the sky speaks.

53.

I gather a stick the length of a man, thrusting it in front. Blind, still seeing the sun, orbed with black constellations, I tap a rock, edge a serrated fern. Beginning to forget what has burnt; beginning to hold what I can't see; beginning to step.

54.

I stand in disappearance. The ground is warm, bees carry pollen across the long green—I smell and hear. I am a bird's stutter. My hair holds shells Ariadne set there, her long fingers entangling them. I gather the world's invisibility like a black gem.

55.

I don't know the mermaid, yet surely I know her: a tenseness of fingers, an indent on her thighs, her rushed speech falling like water. I seek the right words but my mouth gabbles nonsense.

56.

Past the meniscus of sky and land I become
my own ghost. I crave flight, reject it. I'm a
shimmy in a mirror of air. Having dropped
me from freedom, the sun doesn't know me.
I'm no longer Íkaros; I have no other name.

57.

On grass, next to a piping shepherd, tepid light blinds me, who gathered the sun. Bland thought bumps each impress of feeling. Father, Ariadne, childhood, dance-floor. That is myth; I never knew it. That is memory; I was never present. That is knowledge; I can't address it. Grass studies my feet.

58.

Over weeks and months I'm spoken again and begin to see. The mermaid's language undresses me and, in using it like a prop, I pull myself up. Low fields slink towards a canal. I straighten shoulders, facing the wind-stream.

59.

My body can barely gather its feeling. A building juts like the letter 't'; soldiers patrol the battlements. My body disbelieves its memory. Without the cup on the wide table, without wine, without the capable hands of slaves my gestures are insecure.

60.

The Minotaur whispers his name, asking for mine, but I cannot speak. In fields where grain fattens, I sift soil with fingers and wonder what five more wingbeats would have brought.

61.

I was an eagle in freefall. I shook away every name I knew into body and wind. Yet the city's walls and towers stiffened before me, the sound of wailing, my mother's tight-handed gestures. The threshers of grain stood before me, and women who dyed cloth. The fruit pickers with full baskets, honey sellers with dripping wax. And fish like hardenings of silver water. Rat catchers and traders in coin. I was a mouse in undergrowth, a twitching at the end of an eye-beam, a partridge in my father's talon.

62.

I become a searcher of shorelines, speaking in alien accents, seeking new words in sketches of sand, pulling on air like a change of clothes, probing what the flushed sun hides—a shelf of darkness. I see my father tumbled in soil, but flaming with brilliance.

63.

On a tall statue there are shreds of myself. In alleyways I recollect the long descent. A woman approaches but her eyes show nothing clear. In the arena a bull staggers and falls, thread trickling from its lips. What did my father say, pushing me from the window?

64.

Beachcombing, I find my face—a mask that has floated with a shipwreck's detritus. Who knew me so well to make of my face this inscrutable gesture? The sun's rays are stretched tears. Morning opens a chasm of self. The sheep in the paddocks announce a Cyclops. Every tree is a nymph escaping distress. And there is my body cocooned in a shell.

65.

The book is pulp in my hands. The pages are marked; urchins and snails have made home in the spine. (I found it by diving to the wreck of my crash.) Dried, its poems are a strange surrealism. Yet I turn to them, on salted papyrus, to read what water has written of love (not much, it seems, yet I divine what I can from a fragment of Sappho and an anonymous lyric). Words solace a world where centipedes crawl in the rub of dark soil. I see myself flying near the crook of the heavens—but that's just a poem erased by water.

66.

It was not the absence of flight, or the sun's red distance, or my father's labyrinthine words (how I loathe and love and remember them). It was not blown dust or the way white roads pierced hills, gathering a sense of elsewhere. It was a necklace of words; utterance like waves and beach-tossed stones.

67.

Not to be in air or to straddle the void of myself. Not to clamber on the thresh of wings. Not, now, to be Íkaros. Never again to wrap that name in my mouth, remembering the Minotaur, who chose not to kill me. I would know the exquisite terror, lift into his scrawls and jabber, hold my fear as steady as that bull head.

Íkaros as refugee

68.

If I'm not Íkaros, what did my mother call me in her intimate murmurings? If Íkaros is my second name, what is the heavy noun I carry, that drags me to ground? If I possess another story, why isn't it written in these limbs? If the caress of language has hold, why does it feel like abrasive wind?

69.

I stretch arms, reach backwards and my body opens like a row of sardines. Ariadne's in my guts like an evisceration.

70.

Officials take me to a camp with hundreds of refusals. I fall into memory, squat in this terminus. Guards' words are twists of wire.

71.

Then, without flight; without sun flare; without my large dream; without Daedalus or Naucrate; without my own tongue and accent; without whitewash on walls and the scrimmage of games; without the familiar markets; without books I had learnt or objects kept (those pearly shells, that spar of driftwood); without even the rain falling slant from the sea—so I stand in my improbable name and try to answer for who I am.

72.

They are ghosts: Pasiphaë, Ariadne, the Minotaur, Minos. Their kingdom is under water. A weird dream took me there—flat cakes of light, a falling boy, too many stairs. A skirt dropped on stones. I clambered on hilltops and coveted the sea, but my nostrils lost the salt of the climb. Executioners passed with a severed head—an old school mate, smiling a threat. I stood near a fountain and was as tall as my father. The sky bled like a man.

73.

My father's tenderness returns, his milder words like polished quills of light. He's an intimate flare, burning me with his gestures, carrying my other name in his mouth—if only I could remember it. He arrives at night as lightly as a dream, saying 'we'll set off tomorrow'.

74.

Tomorrow, yesterday, today. So many millennia and still the boy breasts the air, feeling immersion as time's sucked away; as the sun baubles brightly; as the mermaid climbs. I'd try it again, strap elaborate wings, hold my father again as he ties me closely. His words breathe on my face as he manoeuvres the waxwork. After all these years, I'm almost ready.

Afterword

The poem Íkaros (a form of the Greek spelling) is an expression of my longstanding interest in the influential Icarus story and, more generally, in the contemporaneity of ancient Greek (and Cretan) mythology. Many writers and artists have responded to the Icarus myth and its powerful group of characters and linked narratives, involving the figures of Daedalus, Theseus, Ariadne, the Minotaur, Pasiphaë, King Minos and others. The idea of Icarus flying too close to the sun has become deeply symbolic as it has accrued myriad different meanings and understandings. Whereas Robert Graves in *The Greek Myths* tries to find the origins and significance of ancient mythological stories in spiritual and cultural practices belonging to the distant past, I am interested in the contemporary resonances and ramifications of such mythologies and the way in which, as they persist through time, they accrete new meanings. In this mythology, the past tense is also the present and future tense, and it speaks as potently for the twenty-first century as it does for the ancient world— although we would benefit from listening to it especially closely. Many mythological stories represent a foreshadowing of insights by 20th- and 21st-century philosophers and physicists who reveal that the common sense understanding of time flowing in one direction, like a river, is mistaken. This poem reinscribes a small but well-known part of the extant inheritance of ancient mythology through exploring the notion that Íkaros lives simultaneously in the ancient and modern worlds, and inside and outside human memory.

Acknowledgements

I would like to express my gratitude to Shane Strange for suggesting publication of this extended poem. In proposing its publication he brought it into being. I'm also very grateful to those who helped me edit the text, primarily Cassandra Atherton—and Paul Munden read the manuscript with great perceptiveness. More generally, I'd like to record my thanks to Andrew Melrose and Jen Webb for rekindling my early interest in the Icarus story, and to the International Prose Poetry Group for providing a forum for the early drafts of many of these poems. And a special thanks to Recent Work Press and all who fly with her.

Biographical note

Paul Hetherington is Professor of Writing in the Faculty of Arts and Design at the University of Canberra, head of the International Poetry Studies Institute (IPSI) and one of the founding editors of the international online journal *Axon: Creative Explorations*. He has previously published eleven full-length collections of poetry—most recently *Burnt Umber* (UWAP, 2016) and *Gallery of Antique Art* (RWP, 2016)—along with six poetry chapbooks. He won the 2014 Western Australian Premier's Book Awards (poetry) and was commended in the 2016 Newcastle Poetry Prize, shortlisted for the international 2016 Periplum Book Competition (UK) and shortlisted for the 2017 Kenneth Slessor Prize for Poetry. He was awarded one of two places on the 2012 Australian Poetry Tour of Ireland, and undertook an Australia Council for the Arts Literature Board Residency at the BR Whiting Studio in Rome in 2015-16. He has an abiding interest in the visual arts and edited the final three volumes of the National Library of Australia's authoritative four-volume edition of the diaries of the artist Donald Friend. He has conducted research into, and edited special journal issues about, ekphrastic poetry and prose poetry, and he formed the International Prose Poetry Group in 2014.

2016 Editions

Pulse **Prose Poetry Project**
Incantations **Subhash Jaireth**
Transit **Niloofar Fanaiyan**
Gallery of Antique Art **Paul Hetherington**
Sentences from the Archive **Jen Webb**
River's Edge **Owen Bullock**

2017 Editions

A Song, the World to Come **Miranda Lello**
Cities: Ten Poets, Ten Cities **Various**
The Bulmer Murder **Paul Munden**
Dew and Broken Glass **Penny Drysdale**
Members Only **Melinda Smith** and **Caren Florance**
the future, un-imagine **Angela Gardner** and **Caren Florance**
Proof **Maggie Shapley**
Black Tulips **Moya Pacey**
Soap **Charlotte Guest**
Isolator **Monica Carroll**
Íkaros **Paul Hetherington**
Metamorphic: 21st Century Poets Respond to Ovid **Various**
Work & Play **Owen Bullock**

all titles available from

www.recentworkpress.com

RECENT
WORK
PRESS

www.ingramcontent.com/pod-product-compliance
Lightning Source LLC
Chambersburg PA
CBHW032046290426
44110CB00012B/969